This Book Belongs to the

Library of

_____

TRUE WORSHIP
TRUE WORSHIPERS

JOHN D. MCDONALD

Cover Graphics and Fonts by Digitaljuice.com

Cover design by Kingdom Living Media

Cover Picture " Rising Crescendo"

All Scripture quotes KJV unless otherwise noted.

ISBN-10: 0615850170

ISBN-13: 9780615850177

ENDORSEMENTS

In his groundbreaking new book, *"True Worship, True Worshippers,"* John McDonald shares liberating insight for ruling and reigning as true sons and daughters of the Kingdom of God. John kicks over "sacred cows" and boldly challenges clichés that have enslaved Christians for years. You will be blessed, encouraged, and empowered by this timely book.

Carlton Reed, Author, *Weapons of Mass Production, 21 days to Uncommon Productivity with God*

With Biblical depth and keen insight, this book by John McDonald brings forth the true depth of worship in the purest form.`

Pastor **Angela Probst, *New Life Ministries, Northumbria PA***

I love to listen to John McDonald teach because he always imparts in me a hunger to search God's Word and a confidence that my search will be rewarded with fresh insight. He has a contagious love for the Word of God and a determination to see minds renewed by Biblical truth. I know that whether or not I agree with everything he says, he will challenge me to make sure my thinking is rooted in the Scriptures and not in the wisdom of man, no matter how popular or conventional. In this book John combines his passion for developing a biblical mindset with his desire to see the church worship her God in Spirit and in truth, not settling for anything less than the full biblical vision of worship.

Joshua Nickel, Author, **A *Life lived For You*** and **The *Righteous Will Live By Faith.***

John McDonald has been a Christian for many years. His experience of walking with Jesus and serving Him to date is enriched with deep passion to see himself and the Body of Christ as a whole, live and demonstrate the resurrection power of God's Kingdom in every facet of life through TRUE WORSHIP. This book is designed to provoke a passion for personal, true worship of our Lord and King. Let the Holy Spirit enable you to receive and practice the revelation of biblical worship as stated in John 4:23-24.

Robert Crenstil, apostle, *Doxa Global Ministries. Washington D.C.* Author; *Turn the Battle To the Gate*

DEDICATION

This book is dedicated to all who desire to worship Father in spirit and in truth.(John 4:24)

As this author expresses in this work worship is obedience. Obedience not out of fear of being intimidated by Him, or believing we must obey or we'll get the big stick and pulled into line.

Rather our fear of God is in fact, to be awe. As the song states, "I stand in Awe of Him". This awe that realizes that love is first expressed by God to us, for it is He who first loved us, This in fact is what the Scriptures means when it speaks of returning to our first love. He created us to be loved and to love. His love does not diminish when we fail, nor does it increase when we succeed.

I stand amazed that the God that created us is the same one that is known to us as the singing God, as Zephaniah tells us; ***"The LORD thy God in the midst of thee [is] mighty; he will save, he will rejoice over thee with joy; he will rest in his love, he** will joy over thee with singing."* Zeph.3:1

CONTENTS

Acknowlegdements..................... 9

Foreword...............................11

Introduction 15

1. How Did We Get Here 19

2. Understanding Glory................ 29

3. What Worship Is Not 41

4. What Worship Is 49

5. The Power of Obedience............ 65

6. Biblical Examples of Worship........81

Conclusion............................ 89

Appendix A O.T. Worship Verses... 97

Appendix B N.T. Worship Versess...109

John McDonald

ACKNOWLEDGEMENTS

First I must acknowledge my thankfulness to my Lord for placing in my heart the hunger and thirst to study and understand Your Kingdom; it has and will continue to be my life's journey.

It is with a very greatful heart that I want to thank those who have over the years encouraged me to write. To my eldest son John who so long ago said "dad you should write a book" while this first book is not the subject in mind, it is still a mile stone in my life. So John even though you probably thought this would never happen, it is important to acknowledge the encouragement you gave me that day.

True Worship True Worshipers while it is one of the eight or so books that are in various stages of completion on my computer, it is the first finished and published, the other will be finished in due season.

To Robert and Connie Brocco two awesome friends that have helped keep me focused. Rob along with Joshua Nickel, and John Loewen have been a great help in editing, what a job.

And last but not least, thanks to all those who have sat under my teaching and have purchased my Cd's; you have kept me going through the those times when we wondered where our next dollar would come from. Even this book was due to someone out of the blue asking for some teaching material that enable me to go to press.

My prayer is that each and every one of you will be vessels of worship that will usher in a greater manifestation of His presence.

FOREWORD

The most critical question that every Christian needs to ask is the one that Jesus asked His disciples in Caesarea Philippi - ***"But who do YOU say that I am?"*** (Matthew 16:15). Unless we have a personal revelation that Jesus is the true, living God, we simply end up having head knowledge *about* Him rather than a life transforming encounter *with* Him. This can lead us into being busy and follow the mechanics of grams. However, when someone has a heart revelation of the majesty, glory, sacrifice, and victory that was accomplished by our King on the Cross, there is something within us that drives us to express our gratitude, love, obedience and service to the King of kings. We desire through the passion of our personal relationship with Jesus to worship and praise Him each day of our lives for what He has done.

So then, how do we worship and praise Him? I often think about how King David would dance and sing before the Lord. He was passionate about God and used dance and song to express his heart.

Dancing, singing, and music in and of themselves are not worship. If it is simply an act of producing a movement, tune or lyrics, then all it does is stir emotions, or worse, an activity of religious ritual.

Emotions and ritualism can be deceiving, but when emotions are borne out of a heart of passion and love in our relationship with Jesus, they become a vehicle to let out what our heart is feeling. If the true believer lives a life of true obedience, and loves as we are commanded, then each one of us will express our heart of worship in the manner that best fits our life and personality.

John has a tremendous heart for God's Kingdom. He desires for people to not play church, but to become the living **ekklesia** of Christ so as to manifest His Kingdom here on earth through each one of our lives. In this his first published book, John endeavors to lay down what he has come to understand what the Biblical idea of worship is. My hope is that it will provoke you the reader to explore this issue of true worship for yourselves so that it becomes revelation to you.

In so doing, my prayer is that it develops a deepening personal heart and desire so that you will delight in expressing your heart felt love and thankfulness towards the One who saved us.

Robert Brocco.

INTRODUCTION

I am writing this book to address what I see as error in the Body of Christ; not intentional error, but error that has been the result of following the traditions of men rather than Scripture. Sometimes, doing something and calling it worship actually leads to problems in other areas of our walk. I believe worship is a case in point and is especially true in the area of His Vineyard that is part of my spiritual heritage since the age of 12, the Pentecostal / Charismatic world. I had never really seen the whole picture till about the last ten years, and increasingly I have been endeavoring to develop a Hebraic mindset and coming to understand the Kingdom in far greater measure.

I realize many, especially those in the area of musical leadership, may not grasp what I am endeavoring to proclaim this difficulty is the result of certain mindsets which has perpetrated within the Church the World's system of education which leads to the dumbing down of God's people.

Certainly there is no grudge against music in my heart; I love music. I love to sing, including songs that give me, as they say, the "goose bumps". Maybe some will think I have a grudge against people who are gifted to lead God's people into His presence; again the answer is no! I too have been involved in that gifting.

I remember the time that I was leading "worship" as I had been taught to understand it, in a service back at the church I was attending in Lilydale, Australia. The church was a well-known Christian fellowship. As I was leading the praise time one Sunday morning and out of the blue I heard this is your last time in leading the Praise time. Even today some cannot understand why I won't do so. This obviously is subject to change if He gave me the permission to do so.

It is now, as I write the introduction to this

material which was originally written in response to a question by a young pastor friend of mine, some four years ago, that I understand why. I was given this direction, it is simply because He wanted me to be an instrument to help bring change to how we understand what worship really is Biblically, and bring true worship back to the forefront of all we do.

I know that to be re-educated is the hardest form of education, because we learn to express ourselves through the paradigm of what we have been taught to think, and changing our way of thinking is worse than reprogramming a computer, because our minds are a living thing, and the computer isn't. The Scriptures, however, tell us very clearly that our minds must be renewed.

The purpose of this book, is to do exactly that, help renew our minds so as to find out what worship really is, according to scripture. We must understand that all things Scripture speaks of come from the foundation of the Kingdom of God and Father's original intent for mankind.

We need to get rid of "religion" and start living Kingdom Life and the manifesting God's presence as Paul wrote to the Colossians in 1:27, unveiling Christ in us in the sphere of influence He has placed us in the world around us.

1

HOW DID WE GET HERE

Have you ever stepped back and wondered, how did we get here, or have you asked yourself that question in regard to something that seems to be the norm yet you don't have the answer to it.

Back in Australia we used to have service at 11 am on Sunday morning, it seemed the 'right' thing to do. But was there any spiritual significance? Then we found out that the farmers used to go out and milk the cows, come back to the house, have breakfast, have a shower or bath, and get ready for church, all before arriving at church by 11 o'clock. In other words, the starting time had no special spiritual meaning, but was simply the result of what had been done on Sundays for generations. Hence the tradition set in;

people forgot why, but nobody was willing to change.

It reminded me of a story I heard many years ago about a new bride, let us call her Jan, who wanted to cook her first roast lamb dinner for her husband. So after buying the leg of lamb, she dressed it. Just before she put it in the roasting dish, she proceeded to chop off a part of the leg. Her husband, we (will call him Jim), seeing this asked her why she was cutting off the end.

She told her husband, "well that is what mum always did".

He responded again with another "why?" She said "I don't know. I'm having lunch with mum tomorrow, so I will ask her".

The next day at lunch, she told her mother about the roast lamb dinner she had prepared, and mentioned that Jim asked her why she had cut off part of the leg, "I told him that was how you did it, but I did not have an answer as to why you did". Her mother told her it was because that is what her mother had done.

To make what could be a long story short, Jan called her grandmother and asked why she cut the leg off the lamb before putting it into the dish and into the oven.

Granny responded, "well because your great grandmother did so";

But why? Jan asked again. Her grand-mother responded," Mum cut off part of the leg because the leg of lamb was too big for the pan".

Most people just accept as normal the way things are done, but then some of us are not satisfied with the status quo. We want to know why? So in pursuing the subject of this book on worship, we can ask the question of why we do 'worship' the way we do, and most likely will not find an answer, because it is more than likely hidden way back in the latter first or second century as the church saw the influx of the Greco-Roman world which led to it becoming institutionalized. This is really beyond the scope of this book, and would be better suited to those who think more like a historian.

We can however ask the question "What does Scripture itself say about worship"? As we seek to see if what we call worship really comes from a Biblical Worldview, or what I call "the Kingdom Worldview", or is simply man centered. I am convinced that Scripture is where we must begin to find the answer. Why? Because Scriptures from Genesis 1:1 to Revelation 22:21 is all about the King and His Kingdom. Worship is primarily the function of Kingdom centered people, who bow to honor the King, seeking first the Kingdom of God and His righteousness. In subjection to Him, they find their Kingdom assignment/s as they are walking out their lives, empowered to manifest His Kingdom in all they do.

Let me state again, Worship is central to understanding the culture of kingdom or the monarchial rule and what it is from the Word of God, so understanding Kingdom is central to understanding worship. Solomon said it well when he said,

"The fear of the LORD is the beginning of knowledge: but fools despise wisdom and

instruction." (Proverbs 1:7)

When I am teaching on leadership and moves of God, I often use two illustrations in relation to the importance of the need to keep re-evaluating what we believe and how we function. The two pictures I use come out of two sayings of Jesus, which even though I have done so many times over the last decade, I have not yet heard anyone else bring them both together to teach how to accommodate the new thing that God wants to do.

The first idea comes from the parable of the wineskins:

"Neither do men put new wine into old bottles: else the bottles break, and the wine runs out, and the bottles perish: but they put new wine into new bottles, and both are preserved." Matthew 9:17

The second is the statement about a wise man:

"Then said he unto them, Therefore every

scribe which is instructed unto the kingdom of heaven is like unto a man that is a householder, which brings forth out of his treasure things new and old." Matthew 13:52

Looking at the first saying, Jesus is telling us that anything new cannot fit into an old structure. The structure prevents the new from reaching its full potential. As the new is trying to do so, it ends up destroying the old wineskin and the new thing is wasted. Notice that Jesus never says the old bottles are no longer valid, but that they need renewing so as to become flexible. The second teaching statement of Jesus confirms the value of both new treasures and old.

Here is my understanding of these two passages; when the Spirit of God begins to move in a new way we need to lay aside our old structures and strictures so as to allow the full measure of all that God wants to do. When we become established in the new, we then look back to what we had, to see what can be brought into the new to give it greater strength. Remember the old treasures can always enhance the new, and the clue is to see what the old treasures are and what is simply nothing more than nostalgia. For that which does not fit is no longer a treasure.

The sad reality is that when we as leaders in the Church see God doing a new thing, we go and search it out, and we endeavor to try and fit it into our structure. What happens is that either the new work of the Spirit dies and or the church breaks. This is why most revivals never seem to last, the people get disillusioned and leave, or when the Spirit begins a new thing down the track, and the people who stayed think. 'Here we go again', 'been there, done that, got the T-shirt and the video,' and so they won't get involved.

Let us look at this in the context of revival. One thing I have learned being involved in a studying revival is this; you cannot begin a revival, but you sure can stop it. If we try and start a revival it means we have in our mind what we are looking for, therefore we have the agenda. Revival is a sovereign work of God, based on His agenda.

If we try and direct Revival, we are controlling

it. As leaders, our role is not to direct it but we are to let it find its direction, for God knows where He wants it to go, we are to stabilize and let it go where He determines. A good example is a river or stream: it finds its own direction. Once it has made its path, we just come behind the head and strengthen the banks on the side.

Another illustration that I think is relevant here is the launching of rockets into space, either manned or unmanned. In having a target in mind, they find the time-frame in which the vessel is to be launched. It is called a launch window. If the launch is done outside the window it will miss its objective. If it is launched with a fraction of a degree off target, even though it may not seem much, the rocket can miss its target by thousands, if not millions of miles. So too with the way we understand the Word or ideas in the Word.

We may be a little off track, but the next generation adds their understanding to it, then the next generation does the same until what started out looking like biblical truth no longer bears any resemblance to the Scripture, let alone truth.

In closing this chapter, I know that there is so much more of God available to us. When I came to understand the Kingdom, I had people ask me this question. "Are you Kingdom now or Kingdom future"? I would simply reply, YES! Then if asked to explain, I would say the Kingdom is here now and it will be in future. I now know that it is simply sitting on the fence. It also takes the responsibility off me and puts it on God.

Today my answer is different, because I know there is far much more of God for us to tap into; and I know that the work of Christ is finished or accomplished. The question is not how much of the Kingdom is here, for the Kingdom is here in full measure. The question is how much of the Kingdom am I willing to tap into and appropriate so that the Kingdom will be manifested through me for His glory.

I am convinced that as we rediscover what the Biblical understanding of worship is, and enter into true worship, then we will become true

worshipers that we will have greater manifesta-
tions of the Kingdom, in and through, our lives.
There is so much more that Father has available
for us. So much more than we can even conceive
off.

2.

UNDERSTANDING GLORY

In Chapter One I addressed some areas where we, the **ekklesia** get off track. "Here is another example of how we get off track, that being what I call "buzz words". Suddenly a particular word becomes the "in word". As God brings a revelation about something to a few, suddenly everyone is either talking about or using the "new word", which may have been used before, but now it is simply taking on a new popularity.

Why I say "off track" is because most likely the majority of those who get caught up in the 'buzz word' don't really have any understanding as to the depth of what is contained in it. It is like the majority would rather want to wade in the shallows of what is, whilst the few capture the great revelation that God is trying to bring us into. For example; in the circles that I am connected with, some have called me a Kingdom scholar. Now, the word Kingdom is used so much more than ever before, yet many who use the word don't have any real understanding of what Kingdom in the Biblical sense means.

I remember back in the early 70's as the "Prophet" became the new ideal, and suddenly every man and his dog became a "prophet".

Then in the 90's those who were satisfied with either being called pastors or prophets before were now calling themselves apostles. Then some who called themselves apostles wanted to trump other apostles so they became 'chief' apostle or 'apostle of love' or some other title to add to their former titles. Others added Dr. to their name and now it was Rev. Dr. Apostle, without a clue that apostleship is a promotion to servanthood rather than being the top dog! But again that is a subject for another time, I am sure you get my drift.

And so we seem to see words come up that

we seldom, if ever, have heard before, let alone understood. One of those words is 'glory'. Apart from a general reference from Scripture and an occasional mention in a sermon, suddenly it seems that every second word is "glory", or "you have the glory all around you". Someone has goose-bumps and they declare "I have the glory". "Glory" it is said by some, is an atmosphere or some other feeling. Of course for many years, glory was a simile for Heaven, so when one spoke about Colossians 1:27, it was about the surety that we will go to Heaven: "Christ in you" was your assurance of going to Heaven. However, the context reveals no such thing, for it is about the glorious hope that the nations would be partakers in the promise that Israel thought was only theirs.

> *"To whom God would make known what is the riches of the glory of this mystery among the Gentiles; which is Christ in you, the glorious hope:"* (Colossians 1:27)

So what is glory in the Biblical sense? To understand the idea imbedded in the concept of glory, we need to go back to the creation account of mankind. We see that God said,

> **"And God said, Let us make man in our image, after our likeness:....... So God created man in his image, in the image of God created he him; male and female created he them. And God blessed them, and God said unto them, Be fruitful, and multiply, and replenish the earth, and subdue it: and have dominion over the fish of the sea, and over the fowl of the air, and over every living thing that moves upon the earth".** (Genesis 1:26-28)

When it comes to the actual process of the creation of man, both male and female we need to look at Genesis 2:7;

> **"And the LORD God formed man of the dust of the ground, and breathed into his nostrils the breath of life; and man became a living soul".** (Genesis 2:7)

We see that God, rather than speaking man into existence, actually forms him, male and female man, in one body formed from the dust of the ground with His own hands. We know because God reveals Himself to Jeremiah in Jeremiah 18 as a potter. We also know as Isaiah tells us that man was created to house the glory, to be His temple, a dwelling place on Earth so to speak.

> **Even every one that is called by my name: for I have created him for my glory, I have formed him; yea, I have made him.** Isa 43:7

So when God forms man from the dust, He then breathes into man the breath of life, or as the Hebrew word shows the word 'life' is plural meaning three or more kinds of life. God, as Father, Word, and Spirit now dwell in Adam and Adam becomes a living soul. Sometime later, as Adam begins his Kingdom assignment, God declares that it is not good for man to be alone. Was he alone? After all, the living God was now dwelling in him. This reveals that God made us with an empty place that can only be filled by someone of our own humanity, an opposite and different, but equal who would be the help meet to be able to accomplish our kingdom mandate, so He took the feminine, the inner being out of the man and formed the woman. When God brings the Adam woman that He had formed to Adam man, he seeing she was him, flesh of my flesh and bone of my bone. Then the Scripture declares they were both naked and not ashamed.

There is something that is revealed when we contrast the statement "they were naked and not ashamed" in Genesis 2:25, and the revelation from their eyes being opened that they were naked in chapter 3:7, 10, 11 of Genesis. After Adam's disobedience to his Father, the presence of God left and their eyes were opened, which is simply declaring they saw something that they never had seen before. They saw they were naked. What was the difference in the nakedness between Genesis chapters 2 verse25 and 3 verse 7?

The clue is found in Genesis 3:8. They heard the voice of the Lord walking in the garden in the cool of the evening, and they were afraid and hid themselves. Why were they afraid? I put it to you that they had never ever heard God's voice in the garden, or had never heard God's voice externally before. They had always heard the voice of the Lord within their spirit, the presence of God in their spirit brought life to their soul, which energized their bodies.

It was not when the wife of Adam ate that things changed, it was after what the man Adam did that caused everything to change. When Adam ate of the fruit, the indwelling presence of God left, and man was dead that day. It was a covenant or spiritual death, and in that state man dies. From that time till after the sacrifice of the Lamb of God that dealt the death blow to the sin problem, God could not live **_in_** the house built for Him, so He waited till a man called Moses arrives on the scene of history, and is commanded to build a temple so He could dwell **_among_** His people.

Now let's move forward in time to the revealing of the Word in human flesh. "The Last Adam" as Scripture calls Jesus, near the end of His human ministry; declares in John 17 this statement;

> **_And the glory which you gave me I have given them; that they may be one, even as we are one:_**" (John 17:22)

What was the 'glory'? It is very clear from scripture that the glory was nothing less than the manifested presence of God in Jesus. Did not Jesus say to the disciple, in other places, 'have I been with you so long yet you have not seen the Father', or 'I and the Father are one', yes even 'I am in the Father and the Father is in me'.

We must remember that the Last Adam reveals to us how the first Adam was to live.[i] The Last Adam lives with the glory, "the manifested presence of God" dwelling in Him This glory was the first Adam, until his act of disobedience. The glory departed and therefore man was naked. The glory, God's manifested presence, is the light that illuminates the image of God in man. When the glory departed the image of God dwelt in darkness, was dead and in that state was dying over time. When we come to Christ we are a new creation man in whom God's spirit dwells, to illuminate the image of God.

We know from the study of Scripture that God is omnipresent, meaning He is everywhere at all times. There is nowhere that He is not. Yet we go to the church building and come away disappointed that God did not show up, so we say the service was dead, but Jesus said; *"where two or three are gathered in my name there am I in the midst"*.

There is an interesting verse I came across some years ago. It shows us the difference between the presence of God, and His manifested presence. It is where God declares I removed the knowledge of my presence. Did you see that? It does not say He removed His presence, just the knowledge of it! I remember back when my oldest son was taking his first steps, and he was really excited as he looked around so proud of his great achievement and saw us watching him. One day as he was continuing to find he could take more steps my wife and I tiptoed out of the room to hide our presence, yet we could peek around the corner and watch his every step. Suddenly he looked up, and not seeing us started to get upset. Had we removed our presence? No, we simple removed the knowledge of our presence. The word 'glory' reveals something far different than His omnipresence, and that difference is that God reveals Himself, and that is called 'His manifested presence', His presence becomes tangible.

I like the way it is expressed by Dutch Sheets when speaking on the glory.

"The Hebrew word for glory is *'kabowd'* which means heavy or weighty. This speaks of the concept of authority. We still use the picture today when we refer to someone who carries a lot of weight. Adam carried that weight, or authority on the earth. He represented God with full authority! He was in charge!"[1]

The Greek word for glory, **doxa,** is just as revelatory. It involves the concept of recognition. More precisely, it is that which causes something or someone to be recognized for what it really is. When creation looked at Adam, they were supposed to see God. And they did! That is until Adam sinned.[2]

Adam was comparable to or similar to God – so much like God that it was illusionary. God was recognized in Adam, which meant that Adam "carried the weight" here on earth. Adam was God's manager here. The earth was Adam's kingdom assignment, it was under Adam's charge or care. Adam was the watchman or guardian. How things went on planet earth, for better or worse, depended on Adam and his offspring.[3]

---

[1] Dutch Sheets, *Intercessory Prayer* (Ventura CA.: Regal Books 1996) p 27

[3] Ibid
3 ibid

When Jesus the last Adam came God was in Him, all He did, said and where He went was manifesting the presence of God in him.

Jesus was "the glory", the manifested presence of God on Earth. Now we, the glory of God are to manifest the presence of God wherever we are appointed to do so. When I was referring to "Christ in you, the glorious hope", from Colossians 1:27, I had this revelation...the sphere we are assigned to, is waiting for 'Christ in us to be unveiled'.

Have you ever noticed it does not say Jesus, but "Christ". Christ was not Jesus' surname, Jesus was His appointment as "the anointed one" in His walk on Earth. The word Christ means "anointed" one and the majority of the Word speaks of function. Simply using the word "anointed" is abstract and as such say's nothing, it leads to error. Looking at the Old Testament, we find certain offices are anointed, such as elders, prophets, priests, and kings. Jesus is the appointed, thereby anointed prophet, priest and king. He was born 'the king' He was not born to be king. And we are the anointed to walk on Earth manifesting God in our sphere of influence in this our time, once we are equipped to fulfill the appointed role we have given.

3

WHAT WORSHIP IS NOT

It is sad that today *"worship"* is demeaned by making it simply about how a "church meeting" is structured; we call it a "worship service". Or it is defined as to the types of songs sung in a meeting: "now we will sing some worship songs". In fact we call the meeting a 'service', where did that idea come from? Maybe to ease the conscience and think that a meeting for 60 minutes or so is serving God, well that doesn't cut it, in my opinion.

Thinking it is about a style of song, that is. songs that are slow and or that make you close your eyes in reverence. So we sing "I Worship You", but singing this song not worship. Of course we employ special ministers we call 'Worship Pastors' of 'Worship Leaders', and we say, we are now going to have "Praise and Worship".

What this simply means is that we have allowed worship to be hijacked by musicians, or center worship around the musicians. I love the type of song that we claim are worship songs just as much as anyone, but it does not portray Biblical worship.

I am in no way trying to put down those whom God has called and anointed to bring us into His presence. Rather I am trying to show clearly that worship has nothing to do with music or singing, to believe so from my understanding of the Scriptures demeans the true character of worship.

How many times do we see advertisements for 'Worship Conferences', or magazines having a particular theme on Worship, yes even magazines that claim to be all about worship, yet every one of these articles, magazines, or adverts are all about music, written by musicians for musicians. Here is another idea from within the Pentecostal-Charismatic world which is my spiritual heritage. We have the idea that walking around with hands raised and speaking in tongues is worship.

This is due to the misreading of John 4:23. *"For the Father is looking for those who will worship Him, in spirit and truth,"* which has nothing to do with tongues. Again please don't get me wrong, I'm not knocking tongues either. I believe in this great gift of the Holy Spirit and have spoken, and continue to speak in tongues since that day when I was twelve years of age and received the Baptism in the Holy Spirit.

What about this; how many times have we done what we as Pentecostal Charismatic's claim is worship, and thereby thinking we are worshiping God, yet we didn't do what He asked us to do yesterday, let alone last week, or last year. If we think just because we "feel good" praying in tongues with our hands raised that God accepts it, then we are mistaken. This isn't worship.

There is a subtle subconscious idea that worship is about making us feel good, I say that because that is what I see, and that is what we have made it with our focus on music or certain songs. The truth is that Worship has nothing to do with making us feel good, it is about making Him look and feel good. About giving Him honor. Let me quote from James B. Jordan, which has some relevance here. Again let me set the background from the story of Adam and Eve that we touched on in a previous chapter.

Adam took something that he was commanded not to. Now please carefully read the story and note, Eve was not even created when God told Adam to touch the tree, to tend the tree, but not to eat of the fruit. So who told Eve she was not to touch it, or consume the fruit? Obviously Adam. Understanding this fact shows why Eve did not die the moment she ate.

Now for James Jordan's statement; *"with the forbidden fruit in his hand, and intending to eat it, Adam could not give thanks to God. Thus, Adam's original sin entailed, among other dimensions, the failure to glorify God as God."*[4]

I see in this the danger that comes with taking something that is set apart solely for the Lord and using it for our own agenda, to build our

---

[4] Primeval Saints. Jordan, James B. p 25, Canon Press, Moscow ID

own ministries or churches, and reputations. How do we do this, we draw attention to man and not God, we put man on a pedestal and what happens? The pedestal is rocked because the ground or foundation upon which it is built is sand, and the pedestal and man on it cannot stand.

This is why I have come to realize that these things are so far removed from what worship is, and have nothing to do with a service or music, or a musician. Worship is so far from these things that it isn't funny. Let me reiterate again I love music, music touches our very souls. I am a soloist and have dreamed about making a CD. I love songs that have solid theology and a tune that touches my heart or moves me, songs that carry an anointing. While I still use the cliché term 'praise and worship' to this day, old habits die hard, don't they. However I am endeavoring to change my words. Because that is not what worship is. I want to find a new way of expressing what we do, so true worship can be released to be what it really is.

Having been involved in and attended many meetings where 'worship' is about the music, now that I have come to understand what True Worship is, I find it so difficult to just be on the sidelines. However I have to understand that those involved have a heart to honor our Lord, and I have to be patient with them because one can only change when something becomes revelation. I can teach all I like and if it is just head knowledge nothing changes, however if it comes from a heart of love, a revelation brings change. Revelation is not taught rather it is caught.

It was just the other day as I was working on the final part of this work that I was in a service where the guest speaker was, as he stated wanting us to worship. He played the sort of songs we call worship songs, and then as it softened he stated, 'come on lets lift our voices in worship', and some other cliché's commonly used to get an audience to 'get with it'. Many times it is simply trying to hype the people up, not that he was, he was sincere. But all this does is bring the attention to the leader, we follow his instructions, it becomes all about him and the service. Again I know this is not the intent of those who lead, but it becomes fact because of the structure we mislabel calling it worship.

When we truly enter into what True Worship is, it becomes about the King and listening intently to His voice, His instructions, we hear no other voice we are suddenly and completely lost to all that is around us. We are no longer insecure for our whole focus is on Him.

4

WHAT WORSHIP IS

Having looked at what worship is not, we now move to what worship really is, not based on religion, or religious ideas, but Biblical truth.

Worship to our Lord and King in the Hebrew is expressed by the word **'shachah'.** Looking in Strong's Concordance the Hebrew word #H7812 **shachah** pronounced **shaw-khaw'** A primitive root; to depress, that is, prostrate (especially reflexively in homage to royalty or God): - bow (self) down, crouch, fall down (flat), humbly beseech, do (make) obeisance, do reverence, make to stoop, worship.

The Greek word also using Strong is the word is **proskuneo** as we find in John 4, when Jesus is talking to the woman at the well. #G4352

proskuneo⁻ pronou-ced **pros-koo-neh'-o** From G4314 and probably a derivative of G2965 (meaning to kiss, like a dog licking his master's hand); to fawn or crouch to, that is, (literally or figuratively) prostrate oneself in homage (do reverence to, adore): - worship.

When we look in Luke's gospel chapter 24:53 it is also the same word as in John 4:24, nowhere is the concept of singing let alone a song that one calls a "worship" song even considered.

So if worship is not about music or singing, what is it?

Firstly, worship has in focus the 'position' of one beginning the act of worship, which is to bow down, to prostrate oneself. In relation to this, I was always taught that we don't do that in church, bow or prostrate, but we do so in our heart. This is just plain nonsensical, as would be 'praise' being done in our heart with nothing coming out of our mouth, or what about giving an offering, I'm giving it in my heart, but putting nothing in the offering plate.

In Psalm 22:3 David speaks of He who *'inhabitest the praises of Israel'*. The word praise has within it the idea of *'high praise'* or praise that has built up to a crescendo. To inhabit has within it the concept of the king *'to be seated'* or *'enthroned'*. Thus the Lord is enthroned on the high praises of His people.

The idea of the king sitting on the throne indicates that He is getting ready to hold audience, and/or to commission one for a task to be done for the king's own pleasure. We need to also note that doing so was done in public, not in private.

When I led the praise times at churches in the past, or teach on what praise is for, I would at times give a concept of what worship was using this visual imagery.

Facing the congregation I would explain saying. "Picture this wall behind me as a moving wall that opens and shuts. As we begin with thanksgiving, then move into praise, we finally arrive at the time when our praise reaches a crescendo, called high praise. This creates an atmosphere wherein we would suddenly see that the wall would open up and there you would see the King on His throne."

Again we must always remember that where two or three are gathered, He is among us. He is here.

However being present in our midst, and manifesting His presence are two entirely different things. How many times do we miss Him manifesting Himself, because we want to get on with the service.

Let me ask, what would you do in that situation? Would you keep singing or would you drop to the floor in homage to Him? Even the weight of His presence would cause you to fall prostrate; we would have no choice.

There is only one answer. If when we understand what worship is, we would fall flat on our faces, prostrating ourselves. We would not move but remain before Him, regardless; the weight or **kabod** of His presence would give us no choice.

We would have no regard as to time, how long it was, because of awe and reverence to Him. There is a popular opinion that we "stand in the glory" that dear reader is so far from being true.

I have come to understand that worship, like all Biblical ideas has three dimensions to it. Example salvation is three dimensional, there is the position or legal status of salvation, **we are saved**, then there is **the working out of our salvation,** as Paul tells us **with fear and trembling,** and finally **the perfection, or maturity or completion** of our salvation.

So to with worship, and so the prostrating of ourselves before the manifest presence of our enthroned King is the beginning or position of worship.

At some point in time He would then say "Arise", still with our head bowed, thus the next action in obedience to His command, and is the continuation, or working out of our worship.

Finally, the King in His command to arise, would also say "Go do", for instance He may say simply "Fear Not" or "Go pack your bags for China", or "go speak to that person in the next isle at the supermarket", I'm sure you get my drift. We then would back out never turning our backs to Him, for that is a sign of disrespect, until we were out of His sight, and in obedience to Him would fulfill our commission, then return bowed with the reward in our hands and lay it at His feet. We are thereby working out our worship.

Here is another question, and I ask this being a pastor. If you were prostrated on the floor at your home church and the Lord told you to arise and go down to *Bill's Gift Store*, and pray for the woman with black hair, in the blue blouse in 10 minutes, would you go or would you stay in the meeting till it is over?

Now let me ask a question for those of us who are or have been pastors or leaders of in the church. What would you think of the person who suddenly gets up off the floor, goes back to their seat, grabs their belongings and leaves the service half way through? Before the tithes and offerings have even been collected, Deacon James asks the person why they are leaving early, to which the person responds, "I have been given an assignment from the Lord". As a leader what would your response be?

I am sure many of us who are leaders would think, as we have been taught that our coming to church is our assignment?

Think about it. What would you do or what would you as a leader think about someone who did just that.

You might be saying, "God would not want us to leave the service, after all I may miss the message, or we haven't taken up the offering yet."

I have come to the conclusion that we have made listening to and obedience to Holy Spirit, conditional upon what else is on, and we miss so many opportunities to listen and then obey, and touch a life with the presence of God, because our mind is more focused on religious ideas than on God's.

In 2002 I was asked to be the interim pastor, for a time of a church in Harrisonburg Virginia. It was at about the three month mark that I shared on what obedience and ministry really is. In the small congregation there were about five families each had their own business. I told them that should we have a revival at the church, and if they had work in their business that needed to be done, they should stay and do what had to be done rather than be at the meetings. I Did this because I believe that the business that they have is their ministry, it is God's business and like Jesus they needed to be about Father's business'.

This is worship in the truest sense. It is the act of obedience to the King and the return, or the reward resulting from fulfilling the assignment in obedience to Him. The problem today is that seldom do we understand that 'obedience' is the result of a heart change, and a renewed mind.

We must also understand that FAITH is never about getting something or obtaining a result; rather FAITH is that which we are given to be obedient. It is the obedience that brings the promised blessing. Blessings come out of obedience, as curses come out of disobedience.

- It is **obedience** that distinguishes the Last Adam from the First Adam.

- It is **obedience,** not sacrifice, that pleases the Father.

- The purpose of faith and/or trust is not so that we can get needs met or be blessed, but rather that we can **obey,** and through our **obedience** receive all we need.

Blessings have nothing to do with what we want, but rather what we need to accomplish our assignments, which at times includes the ability to provide for a brother or sister or family in Christ who God speaks to us to help. That is the very essence of the teaching of Jesus about the Kingdom in His sermon on the mount.

> *"But seek ye first the kingdom of God, and his righteousness; and all these things shall be added unto you".* Matthew 6:33

Now having said that Music or Music leaders, let's call them Ministers of Music, have nothing to do with worship, let me now give you an examples where music and or the Minister of Music has a connection to worship.

Let's call the Minister of Music Timothy. When Father speaks to Timothy to write a song, in doing so it is worship, because it is an act of obedience by him. However the song is not a 'worship song' nor is singing the song, worship. Rather, singing the song is an act of praising Him. Timothy's act of obedience, therefore worship, was to enable the people to build their level of praise so as to usher in the Glory or the manifested presence of God, where all will fall prostrate before Him. Notice that it is all to bring attention to the presence of God in the midst, not attention to man, especially the music team.

When the Spirit of God speaks to Timothy who was planning to sing "song 3" on his list, to sing a song not on his list for the service, doing so is worship because it is obedience to the Lord's assignment at that time.

However the congregation in singing that song as led by the leader is not worship, rather it is an act of praise by the them.

You may think I am majoring on minors. I would argue however that my heart is about getting us to refocus on what worship really is. For we are all called to worship; we have all been called to obey, as the Word say's. *"if you love Me you will keep my commandments"*.(John 14:15) To keep means to tend to, as one tends to their garden, and His commandments are not grievous to us.

Again let's look at the teaching of Jesus in John 4:23:

> *"For the Father is looking for those who will worship Him, in spirit and truth"*.

The difference between the Old Covenant and New Covenant in regard to worship is this. In the Old Covenant worship or obedience was based external law, the tablets of stone. Whereas, the New, on the other hand, is internal from the heart, for His Law/Word is engraved on our hearts of flesh, because the Living God and King dwells in us not among us. Holy Spirit lives in us so by keeping His commandments we walking by the Spirit, in other words we instantly obey.

Let me digress for a moment, to address what law is engraved on our hearts, the same law engraved on the tablets of stone. The issue is not the law, the issue is about what the law is engraved upon. Remember the law is multi-dimensional, it is first based upon God's righteousness, and secondly it reveals what sin is. What is sin? Anything that does not meet God's righteous standards lived out by faith. I am also convinced that the law written by the finger of God is exactly what Jesus wrote in the sand, when the woman was thrown down at Jesus feet, claiming she was caught in the act of adultery. Jesus said, "he who is without sin cast the first stone" and as He wrote with *"the finger of God"* each commandment they were convicted, dropping their stones and left till there was no one standing there. These would have been the only laws that would convict them.

I have been told that the Hebrew root word for worship is the same as that for work. Thus working for the King, the work for which we were created and gifted for, and functioning in the sphere of authority to which we are assigned to is true worship. I am not sure that this is true, but I am sure of one thing: our work was meant to be our worship. Not works to earn salvation, but working out the salvation we have received, and fulfilling the assignment we were put on earth for, and the time in which we are on earth, so as to be manifesting the Kingdom on earth as it is in heaven. None of us are here by accident, or put here simply to exist. Every one of us are important to our creator, and we have been designed for a purpose.

God never intended for us to work or as we say "get a job" that was not a part of our calling. We are not created to get a job, we are created to have a ministry that will enable us to walk in dominion and reconcile people to God. In many cases what we call our job, in which we are not really happy, can become so if we just have a mind change that enables us say it is the ministry to which God has called us. A simple change thinking can change one from being discontented to being content.

1. The old English word for worship is *"obeisance"*, Winston's dictionary states; that the word is from the French *obeir,* "to obey", meaning 'to bow or a bend of the knee as an expression of, obedience or submission.

2. So worship in spirit and truth is obedience to the work of the Kingdom in our sphere of influence. As one manifests true worship, ones sphere of influence increases. He who can be trusted in the small things will be given much more.

Another thought: how many times have you heard the expression, "the Christian Life is all about Him and nothing of me". It sounds so spiritual, so self-effacing, but in reality, it is a form error. Why? Because He can do nothing without us being available for Him to flow through.

Father created man as a dwelling place for Him to live in and flow through ever since the first Adam was created to be His temple. His temple on earth is exactly what Jesus has accomplished through His dealing with the sin question which began with

Adam's disobedience to His Father, where he became an orphan that his progeny inherited, until God's answer, the Word made flesh came, The last Adam fully man and fully God, who knew no sin, accomplished the Fathers will and restored man back to His original intent, as Peter reveals to be the temple, not of stones but of "living stones", or flesh, which Isaiah refers to when he speaks of a new covenant where God's law word is written on hearts of flesh.

When Jesus walked the earth, it was all about Him and Father. That is what we theologians refer to as the hypostatic union, 100% God and 100% man.

Let me ask this question to those of you who are married.

Is marriage 50/50? I am confident you will agree that it isn't. Is it 100% to your spouse and none of you? Again the answer is no.

The true understanding of marriage is 100% plus 100% to make one flesh, completely yielded as an act of love one to the other. So too, it is with us as believers, totally yielded to Christ Jesus our Saviour, Lord and King, our Bridegroom, totally yielding to Him, so He can flow through you. As Jesus Himself, says; *"If you abide in me, AND I abide in you"* He in you, and you in Him, thereby demonstrating perfect harmony of God and man in complete union.

You cannot tell His people or force His people to worship, just like you cannot tell or force people to submit. They can only do so when they see the King high and lifted up, enthroned in their presence.

5

THE POWER OF OBEDIENCE

"And Samuel said, Hath the LORD delight in burnt offerings and sacrifices, as in obeying the voice of the LORD? Behold, to obey is better than sacrifice, and to hearken than the fat of rams [I Samuel 15:22].

After I had this book published, a pastor friend told me he thought I would have used the above passage in it. I did not because I was endeavoring to write what the Lord had impressed me to write. To simply write something simply because of a suggestion by someone else, is not how I work. However as I began to meditate on the verse and Holy Spirit began to reveal some things to me. I was impressed to add this chapter on the issue of obedience. So let us discuss this very important verse. The beauty of self-publishing allows us as writers to publish and change as we develop without having to spend thousands of dollars upfront or having to sell thousands of copies of our work before we can do any rewriting.

This is where we get the quote "obedience is better than sacrifice". Actually this verse did not even come to mind in all the time I spent on writing, revising, and adding to the book. As I have meditated over this verse since my friend wrote to me about his surprise in not mentioning it, I have seen something I have never heard anyone either speak of, or write about in all the years I have been studying the Word of God. Usually it is referred to more in general terms or a text to start a particular message on obedience. I am convinced this one verse contains far more than what we see on the surface. So let us see what we can glean if we dig a little deeper.

We read at the beginning of 1 Samuel 15, that God speaks to Samuel while Samuel is with Saul, telling him that He remembers what the Amalekites did to Israel as they came up from

Egypt. So Samuel tells Saul that he is to totally wipe out the city of Amalek, and every man woman and child, ox, sheep, camel and ass. So Saul gathered an army and did as Samuel commanded him with the Word from the Lord. Or did he?

We find in verse nine that Saul and the people did not do as God commanded, but rather spared Agag, and the best of the sheep, and of the oxen, and of the fatlings, and the lambs, and all that was good, and would not utterly destroy them: but everything vile and refuse, that they destroyed utterly.

Here we find Saul "sparing" all that was good. However, God Himself saw that there was nothing good among the Amalekites, or else God would have commanded what was good to be spared. So Saul disagrees with God, and rebels; disobeying the command of God, the Creator of all that was to be destroyed.

God speaks to Samuel that He repented that He had set up Saul as king of Israel. Better still that He listened to the people of Israel who pestered God to have a king that was like all the nations around about. To give them a king then, rather than waiting until His true choice of a king was in place; one after His own heart to rule Israel. Then, when Samuel comes to Saul, and Saul greets Samuel with a blessing and says we have done all that the Lord commanded us to do, to which Samuel responds, oh really? So what then is this bleating of sheep and the lowing of oxen that I hear?

Notice Saul justifies not just disobedience, but rather his rebellion, which is in reality witchcraft, with a religious excuse that we kept the best to sacrifice unto the Lord.

How often do we justify our disobedience by trying to put religious garb onto the reason we disobeyed?

I see this verse as a double-barrel shotgun that covers issues from the past and the future with one shot.

Let us look at the future issue that comes from this verse. Had Saul obeyed God down to the last letter it would have changed the history we know that happened to Israel. When we look at the book of Esther we find that Israel, being scattered throughout the nations and especially Persia had an arch nemesis, his name was Haman. Haman was appointed as the Prime Minister to Ahasuerus, and he had only one agenda and that was to destroy the Jews scattered throughout all of Persia. Note this was approximately six hundred years after Saul had disobeyed God. You may ask what has Saul's disobedience got to do with Haman. Good question! The answer is that Haman was a descendant of the Amalekites.

Had Saul wiped out everybody as God commanded, Haman would not have come onto the scene. So Saul's disobedience and his rebellion caused a future generation to experience the possibility of being wiped off the face of the earth and their generations after them. When we with our limited view of life and the future, question and disobey God who is omniscient, knowing what the future holds, our disobedience makes it far more difficult for future generations to survive.

There is a real lesson for us looking at Saul's disobedience, and the future and it is this. Whatever battles we refuse to fight today, we make the battle far more dangerous for the future generations to fight. John Piper made this statement, *"we will never know what prayer is for until we realize that LIFE is war."*[5] We only have to look at what happened to Israel when Joshua died. Israel lost the heart to fight to keep what God had given them.

Disobedience today, as in the past, can have a profound impact on our future generations in our family line, and it will also have an impact on our neighbor's family generations. This is what it means by the sins of the fathers are visited three and four generations.

So we need to walk in obedience which is what True Worship is.

---

[5] Piper. John, "Let The Nations Be Glad", Baker Book House Grand Rapids: (1999)

Now looking at this verse from the other barrel of the double-barrel shotgun. This is the revelation I received when meditating on this verse. As I have pointed out previously, the Scriptures clearly contrasts the life of the first Adam who disobeyed, and thus his progeny were to live life in the state of death, devoid of the presence of God within them, with the life of the Last Adam who brought life to all who have Him within.

Now here is something I have never thought of before, nor heard anyone else speak of or write about. Are you ready?

If Adam had obeyed God, there would have been no need for sacrifices of animals, which only covered sin. Nor would there have been any need for God to provide the perfect sacrifice of His only begotten Son, for there would be no sin to atone for.

- God would never have left Adam naked of God's glory by removing Him self thereby man no longer having the glory of God.

- Adam would not have a progeny living an existence of death therefore death would no longer separate man from God.
- Adam's obedience would have taken care of Eve's disobedience. Just like our disobedience, as blood bought believers, are covered by the obedience of our Savior, Lord and King.

God never designed for Adam to disobey, nor has He designed us to disobey. Let me share something from a guest speaker, I heard many years ago in Australia, it was in 1977, at our Assemblies of God Biennial Conference. His name is David Asel. He shared from his book which was called "I Never Set the Grass On Fire", he made a statement that I have never forgotten to this day that relates to two different actions of God: *"The keeping power of God is greater than the delivering power of God"*.

David was sharing how as a Christian from

his early childhood, he as a young man heard a testimony in church of how a guest speaker shared about how God delivered him from this and that, so much so that David started to doubt his salvation, because he had never been involved in any sinful living. One day feeling so low about not having lived in sin, the Lord spoke to him and told him, my keeping power is greater than my delivering power. This set many free that day, and whilst I rejoice in hearing great testimonies of how Father has delivered people from the vilest form of sin in their lives. I rejoice more in those who have never been involved in sexual perversion, drug addiction, or from little crimes to major crimes. I rejoice that God has kept them, as He has kept me from corruption by His keeping power. Paul writes to Timothy about the keeping power of the Lord.

> *"For the which cause I also suffer these things: nevertheless I am not ashamed: for I know whom I have believed, and am persuaded that he is able to keep that which I have committed unto him against*

that day" [II Timothy 1:12].

Obedience is worship; it is True Worship, when we walk in obedience not to external laws written on tablets of stone, but obedience to the law engraved on hearts of flesh, which we can only do as Paul writes to the Romans.

"There is therefore now no condemnation to them which are in Christ Jesus, who walk not after the flesh, but after the Spirit" [Romans 8:1].

Obedience based on tablets of stone, external law is obedience out of duty. But obedience to the law engraved on hearts of flesh, by walking by the Spirit is Worship in Spirit and Truth and is a demonstration of love not duty.

"If ye love me, keep my commandments" [John 14:15]

"If ye keep my commandments, ye shall abide in my love; even as I have kept my Father's commandments, and abide in his love" [John 15:10].

How many times have we heard, "we are not under law but under grace", claiming that we don't have to live by God's laws anymore. For one to use grace as a reason to justify disobedience means that one does not understand grace at all. Let me ask a question;

Did Jesus live by the law. Yes He did, but not out of duty, He did so out of love, as John 15:10 clearly reveals.

Have you ever wondered what Jesus wrote in the sand when the woman that was "caught" in the act of adultery was brought to Him? Ask yourself this question; what would prick them in their hearts causing them to drop their stones and leave. Think about it.

- Jesus was God the Word made flesh.
- Jesus wrote with His finger in the sand.
- Therefore that which was written was written by the "finger of God".
- Moses came down off the mountain, with two tablets of stone that had the 10 words written by the finger of God.

Therefore I am convinced that Jesus wrote the 10 words or as we call them the 10 commandments.

When we are children we obey out of duty because we are learning to obey through the things we suffer. However, when we are Sons we obey no longer out of duty but rather out of love. Love as the foundation of all we do has moved us out of legalism and into grace. We demonstrate our love for God, and we demonstrate out love for our neighbor. Chick-fil-A is a classic example of obeying the 10 commandments out of love rather than out of legalistic law. They close on Sunday, firstly, out of love for God, and also because of their love for their neighbor, the ones who work for them. I know that Sunday is not the Sabbath, for the Sabbath simply means the seventh day. Sunday is the first day. The issue is not law but principle; they give their staff a day off to rest.

This begs the question; what is legalism?

Legalism is blindly following the law out of duty, which does not have any connection to the mind, thinking why am I doing this, or the heart that is only focused only on duty rather than loving God, and thereby not wanting to dishonor Him.

If one reads the Old Testament and how the

Law came into being, one finds that the law is based on love. This is very clear in Deuteronomy, let us take a look.

Hear, O Israel: The LORD our God *[is]* **one LORD: And thou shalt love the LORD thy God with all thine heart, and with all thy soul, and with all thy might(resources). And these words, which I command thee this day, shall be in thine heart:** Deuteronomy 6:4-6

This is why when Jesus was asked what is the greatest of the laws, Jesus quotes from this passage, and with the addition to love your neighbor as yourself.

Jesus lived from the internal Word of God. He did so not out of duty, but out of love. The day John the Baptist declared, *"behold the Lamb of God"*, he, John pronounced the death of God's Son. However Jesus could only die as the Lamb of God, if He was without spot or wrinkle. So Jesus' obedience to God was out of love. His obedience to God was out of His love for all creation, especially for fallen mankind.

It is so important for us to understand that our

disobedience today will have consequences on future generations. On the other hand our obedience today will bring great reward on future generations. That being said, there is a vast difference between the consequences of our disobedience or obedience upon those around us and the generations to come, and the love of God to and for us.

The word "obedience" so often seems to be someone's button that just gets pushed and they go on the rampage of "I am not under law, I'm under grace".

So it is important to understand obedience is never the foundation of all we who are found in Christ Jesus do, LOVE is the foundation, well it is supposed to be.

See; contrary to our experience our with our human fathers and mothers, who are often 'surprised' by the things we do, good or bad, He is not. God is not taken by surprise when we fail to obey, and our failing does not cause Him love us less. Neither does God love us anymore because we succeed. His love remains the same in our failures and in our successes. We can do nothing to make us love God any more than He does, nor any less.

So many of us have had a disaster when it came to our parents.. Either our families broke up so we missed the love of a father, or our parents did not know how to show love. So every form of discipline we see came out of a the concept of punishment, rather than discipline coming out of a heart of love. This then has caused many of us to have a very poor image of God and His love as a true Father. So we always had to perform to be loved. This in turn, is in my view, one of the reasons that we take on a humanistic view of love which sees any form of punishment into a box titled unloving acts.

I came across a comment the other day by Tracy Evans. When I read it, I just had to say WOW. "If He allowed us to stay within our boundaries of fear we would never reach our full potential"[6] To which I add, fear comes about due to our limited view of God. When we have fear we are simply saying no one can get me out of this, or take me through this, so if we include God as one of those who cannot help, then fear over

---

[6] Valloton, Kris. Outrageous Courage, p104 Chosen Books MN

comes us. However, we know that Father can bring us out, or take us through. We put our confidence and love upon Him. As we focus on loving Him, we realize it is because it is He who first loved us. If He first loved us, then we know we have no need to fear, and as John says; "

There is no fear in love; but perfect love casteth out fear: because fear hath torment. He that feareth is not made perfect in love. We love him, because he first loved us. **1 John 4:18-19**

Understanding that He first loved us, is the key to returning to our first love. It simply means that we must come back to the place where we knew He is the one who began the love process. This is so often something we forget and we slip into the slime of performance to earn His favor. And again performance as we know is not something that He is impressed with.

6

BIBLICAL EXAMPLES OF WORSHIP

Two great pictures of what worship is can be found in the Old as well as the New Testaments. In the old we have the dedication of Solomon's Temple. The dwelling place for God on earth that David had in his heart to build, we'll get to that in a moment. The other great example is found in the New Testament at the ascension of Jesus as recorded by Luke. I don't recollect any reference to the disciples or apostles bowing in worship to Jesus accept in the last few moments of His physical presence on earth.

So now let's us go back to the Old Testament, to look at the dedication of Solomon's Temple found in the book of 2 Chronicles.

V1.Thus all the work that Solomon made for the house of the LORD was finished: and Solomon brought in all the things that David his father had dedicated; and the silver, and the gold, and all the instruments, put he among the treasures of the house of God.

Then Solomon assembled the elders of Israel, and all the heads of the tribes, the chief of the fathers of the children of Israel, unto Jerusalem, to bring up the ark of the covenant of the LORD out of the city of David, which is Zion. .....

V. 11 And it came to pass, when the priests were come out of the holy place: (for all the priests that were present were sanctified, and did not then wait by course:

Also the Levites which were the singers, all of them of Asaph, of Heman, of Jeduthun, with their sons and their brethren, being arrayed in white linen, having cymbals and psalteries and harps, stood at the east end of the altar, and with them an hundred and twenty priests sounding with trumpets:)

It came even to pass, as the trumpeters and singers were as one, to make one sound to be heard in praising and thanking the LORD; and when they lifted up their voice with the trumpets and cymbals and instruments of music, and praised the LORD, saying, For he is good; for his mercy endures for- ever: that then the house was filled with a cloud, even the house of the LORD;

So that the priests could not stand to minister by reason of the cloud: for the glory of the LORD had filled the house of God.

Notice that the musicians and singers did not 'worship' but created the atmosphere where worship could take place. In other words they entered into thanks-giving and praise until the praise reached a place that Psalm 2 speaks of as 'high praises', then the 'glory cloud' comes in. The glory cloud is the presence of God manifested in cloud form. So we again ask what is the glory? The glory is not a feeling it is not an idea, it is God manifesting Himself.

Another point to grasp is that when God manifested Himself ALL who were officiating, and all who were in the building at the time God manifested Himself, could do nothing but fall under the weight of God's presence in worship. Let me ask you have you ever been in a meeting where everyone falls on the floor prostrate, including every- one in what we call the worship team. I like Matt Redmond's comment that I heard him say in a Conference in Richmond VA, that goes something like this, "I am not a worship leader, I am the lead worshiper." In other words those who are involved are the first to respond at the manifestation of God's presence. They don't try to get people to follow them. However when we think that worship is about the music team, we follow man and what man thinks should be done, which enforces the importance of man rather than the desire of the Lord.

Jesus said 'seek first the Kingdom of God, and His righteousness", why? Because all God's desires for us, our Kingdom assignment are found in the throne. When we live to seek the Kingdom all we ever need is available to us. However until we come before the throne, boldly to prostrate ourselves before and in silence listen for His still small voice, we'll never achieve the assignment we have been created for.

Finally in looking at Luke's account of the ascension found in Luke 24:51-52

And it came to pass, while he blessed them, he was parted from them, and carried up into heaven.
And they worshipped him, and returned to Jerusalem with great joy:
And were continually in the temple, praising and blessing God. Amen.

First the disciples at their apostolic commissioning Matthew 28:18-20 and Acts 1:8 had already received their assignment. That was to tarry in Jerusalem till they were endured with power from on high.

A side note, have you ever noticed that the disciples were first equipped by the Lord Himself then commissioned with authority and then empowered. We are first empowered with Holy Spirit and then are to be equipped, tested and then released or sent, by someone who knows our heart and call. That is why relationship is of such importance in the process of finding a true Father who will raise us up to be all we can as a true Son.

When we read Luke we see that as they were commissioned, then at the departure of Jesus from the earth realm, hey fell prostrate. When He was no longer visible they arose and continued on the way to Jerusalem to tarry as commanded. This too was worship because this was walking out obedience to Him.

I trust that as you have read this small work that you have grasped that obedience is worship, and it is obedience out of love, not duty, that captures His heart and enables Him to turn His face to you, and in seeing His face you know that you have all you need to do all you are required to do and to build the next generations.

The destiny of our country and the generations ahead will be governed by how we respond to Him in TRUE WORSHIP.

His Disciples asked "Lord, teach us to pray? One line was "Thy will be done as in heaven so in earth. That earth begins in us who are earthen vessel's and then through us who are treasures hidden in earthen vessels to extend the kingdom

of God. To many preachers, churches and theologians have a contrary view of this line in the
Lord's prayer is, "thy will not be done on earth as
it is in heaven.

CONCLUSION

As I stated in the Introduction my purpose is to bring a fresh, yet biblical understanding to the Body of Christ as to what worship really is. Frankly I am wholly dissatisfied with the current widespread definition as I am sure you the reader are as well .

I trust you have understood the intent of my heart in penning these words that you have read and to know that I am not against what happens in "worship" in the way this term is currently used, in fact I want to see more of what we do, and want to be involved in it. But again when we worship in the Biblical way we have so much more to gain, and so much more honor Him with.

I have loved Hillsong music even before it became what it is today, with Geoff Bullock who wrote some awesome songs to the Lord, and has followed on with many song writers that have impacted the nations. Then there is Christian City

Church, also from Australia. Christ For The Nations in Dallas, and City Harvest Church in Singapore who have brought us incredible songs like "The God I Know/The Church He Knows", "Out of My Hands" and many others. Today Dustin Smith of World Revival Church in Kansas City, not to mention Jesus Culture and other great music from forget Bill Johnson's church in Redding California.

I also love to sing and have many soundtracks I use and love, like "We Are Standing on Holy Ground,", "I Stand In Awe of You", and many others. As I have clearly stated, my heart is not about seeing what we have commonly referred to as worship dissipate; rather I want to see it increase with greater intensity. If however as I believe I have shown this is not what worship is, then we need to use some other word to describe what we are doing. To define it Biblically as praise and high praise, and then use the word worship in its true biblical reality, the action of obedience, spontaneous obedience, and here is why.

As the Scriptures speak of warfare, we under

stand we go to war for a very specific purpose as Paul writes to the Corinthian church thus;

> *"but I ask, not being present, that I may be bold with the confidence which I think to be daring against some, the ones reckoning us as walking according to flesh. For walking about in flesh, we do not war according to flesh; for the weapons of our warfare are not fleshly, but powerful to God to the demolition of strongholds, the demolishing of arguments and every high thing lifting up* itself *against the knowledge of God, and bringing into captivity every thought into the obedience of Christ,* (II Corinthians 10:2-5)

Then Paul adds a very important statement the often neglected verse 6, which I believe he takes us back to Psalm 149:

> *"and having readiness to avenge all disobedience, whenever your obedience is fulfilled.* (II Corinthians 10:6)

When our obedience is complete, and Worship is obedience. Obedience to Father hinders the plans of the enemy, in fact as the obedience of the Last Adam reveals, the enemies plans end up in confusion and are exposed for what they are.

Through our obedience, true worship will enable the Gospel of the Kingdom to advance God's Kingdom like never before and Fathers original intent will be restored.

As I have pursued my studies of the Kingdom of God over the years there is a verse that gets mentioned so often yet in my opinion is so often misunderstood. The quote is "***unless you become as little children you cannot enter the Kingdom of God***". Some of the ideas that are espoused are; you have to be child-like, thinking and acting like a child. Yet the scripture says we must put away childish things. Others say a child is teachable, yet many are not.

I am convinced it refers back to Hebrew culture addressing the responsibilities of parents that they are to teach children to be instantly obedient, to be spontaneously obedient. Wanting to please his dad. Let us look at how the Hebrew family worked. A child, especially a male child, was brought up by the mother till the age of twelve to build in the child a soft heart. Then handed over to the father to continue building the lad to have a tough skin and develop him into a man. At the age of thirty, the man if he had proved himself trustworthy was adopted by his father as his son, and from that point he would be given the ring of authority to act on his father's behalf. This is also when he would be handed over to our heavenly Father to act in obedience to His voice as he did to his parents.

Being a teacher of the Word I encourage you to make a lifestyle of defining our words as Scripture defines them, and then let what is properly defined be our lifestyle. Why? Because words describe ideas and ideas have consequences.

This concept of ideas having consequences is no more important than in the area of theology. Your theological ideas will determine how you live; how you live today will determine what your future will hold and manifest.

I want to stress that while we have a lot of 'grace' people who when they hear or see the word 'obedience' seem to have a hissy fit. Because in their understanding obedience is the opposite to grace. That is so totally unscriptural. I am totally convinced that it isn't obedience that is counter to grace, but rather the way obedience is established or is lived out. I ministered once on pleasure where I taught how I came to the place where pleasure contrary to my upbringing was not sin. Yes sin is pleasurable for a time, but them serving Father out of love is also pleasurable. So like pleasure is like obedience, where the problem comes from the path you are walking on. Either the path of God's plans and purposes, see Jeremiah 29:11, or our own path and carnal desires that may be pleasurable for a season but always leads to joylessness.

So obedience that is out of duty is legalism, and legalism is not founded in grace. It is the letter of the law that kill's, what does it kill? It kills your joy, your life.

However obedience out of love, is not legalism and therefore is of grace. Jesus was full of grace, yet He was obedient to the will of the Father even to the death on the cross. In His obedience out of Love for His Father and His will, whatever He did was full of joy for Him.

Therefore there is absolutely no conflict between true obedience and true grace.

The gospel,
The true gospel

'the gospel of the Kingdom'

is the power of God unto salvation

that brings the life of Joy
even in the midst of battle and
what looks like defeat.

APPENDIX A

SCRIPTURE REFERENCES OF WORSHIP
OLD TESTAMENT

*And Abraham said unto his young me; Abide ye here with the ass; and I and the lad will go yonder and **worship**,⁷⁸¹² and come again to you.* (Genesis 22:5)

*And he said unto Moses, Come up unto the LORD, thou, and Aaron, Nadab, and Abihu, and seventy of the elders of Israel; and **worship**⁷⁸¹² ye afar off.* (Exodus 24:1)

*For thou shalt **worship**⁷⁸¹² no other god the LORD, whose name is Jealous, is a jealous God:* (Exodus 34:14)

*And lest thou lift up thine eyes unto heaven, and when thou see the sun, and the moon, and the stars, even all the host of heaven, should be driven to **worship**⁷⁸¹² them, and serve⁵⁶⁴⁷ them, which the LORD thy God hath divided unto all nations under the whole heaven.* (Deuteronomy 4:19)

And it shall be, if thou do at all forget the LORD thy God, and walk after other gods, and serve them, and **worship**⁷⁸¹² them, I testify against you this day that ye shall surely perish. (Deuteronomy 8:19)

Take heed to yourselves, that your heart be not deceived and ye turn aside, and serve other gods, and **worship**[7812] them; (Deuteronomy 11:16)

And now, behold, I have brought the firstfruits of the land, which thou, O LORD, hast given me. And thou shalt set it before the LORD thy God, and **worship**[7812] before the LORD thy God: (Deuteronomy 26:10)

But if thine heart turn away, so that thou wilt not hear, but shalt be drawn away, and **worship**[7812] other gods, and serve them; (Deuteronomy 30:17)

And he said, Nay; but *as* captain of the host of the LORD am I now come. And Joshua fell on his face to the earth, and did **worship**,[7812] and said unto him, What saith my lord unto his servant? (Joshua 5:14)

And this man went up out of his city yearly to **worship**[7812] and to sacrifice unto the LORD of hosts in Shiloh. And the two sons of Eli, Hophni and Phinehas, the priests of the LORD, *were* there. (1 Samuel 1:3)

Now therefore, I pray thee, pardon my sin, and turn again with me, that I may **worship**[7812] *the LORD.* (1 Samuel 15:25)

Then he said, I have sinned: yet honor me now, I pray thee, before the elders of my people, and before Israel, and turna *gain with me, that I may **worship**[7812] the LORD thy God. (1 Samuel 15:30)*

*And this thing became a sin: for the people went **to worship** before the one, even unto Dan. (1 Kings 12:30)*

*In this thing the LORD pardon thy servant, that when my master goeth into the house of Rimmon to **worship**[7812] there, and he leaneth on my hand, and I bow myself in the house of Rimmon: **when I bow down myself** [7812] in the house of Rimmon, the LORD pardon thy servant in this thing. (2 Kings 5:18)*

*But the LORD, who brought you up out of the land of Egypt with great power and a stretched out arm, him shall ye fear, and him shall ye **worship**,[7812] and to him shall ye do sacrifice. (2 Kings 17:36)*

*But if ye say unto me, We trust in the LORD our God: is not that he, whose high places and whose altars Hezekiah hath taken away, and hath said to Judah and Jerusalem, Ye shall **worship**[7812] before this altar in Jerusalem? (2 Kings 18:22)*

*Give unto the LORD the glory due unto his name: bring an offering, and come before him: **worship**[7812] the LORD in the beauty of holiness. (1 Chronicles 16:29)*

But if ye turn away, and forsake my statutes and my commandments, which I have set before you, and shall go and *serve other gods, and **worship**[7812] them; (2 Chronicles 7:19)*

*Hath not the same Hezekiah taken away his high places and his altars, and commanded Judah and Jerusalem, saying, Ye shall **worship**[7812] before one altar, and burn incense upon it? (2 Chronicles 32:12)*

*But as for me, I will come into thy house in the multitude of thy mercy: and in thy fear will I **worship**[7812] toward thy holy temple. (Psalms 5:7)*

*All the ends of the world shall remember and turn unto the LORD: and all the kindreds of the nations shall **worship**[7812] before thee. (Psalms 22:27)*

*All they that be fat upon earth shall eat and **worship**:[7812] all they that go down to the dust shall bow before him: and none can keep alive his own soul. (Psalms 22:29)*

*Give unto the LORD the glory due unto his name; **worship**[7812] the LORD in the beauty of holiness. Psalm 29:2*

*So shall the king greatly desire thy beauty: for he is thy Lord; and **worship**[7812] thou him. (Psalms 45:11)*

*All the land shall **worship**[7812] thee, and shall sing unto thee; they shall sing to thy name. Selah. (Psalms 66:4)*

There shall no strange god be in thee; neither shalt thou **worship***[7812] any strange god.* (Psalms 81:9)

All nations whom thou hast made shall come and **worship***[7812] before thee, O Lord; and shall glorify thy name.* (Psalms 86:9)

O come, let us **worship***[7812] and bow down: let us kneel before the LORD our maker.* (Psalms 95:6)

O **worship***[7812] the LORD in the beauty of holiness: fear before him, all the earth.* (Psalms 96:9)

Confounded be all they that serve graven images, that boast themselves of idols: **worship***[7812] him, all ye gods.* (Psalms 97:7)

Exalt ye the LORD our God, and **worship***[7812] at his footstool; for he is holy.* (Psalms 99:5

Exalt the LORD our God, and **worship***[7812] at his holy hill; for the LORD our God is holy.* (Psalms 99:9)

We will go into his tabernacles: we will **worship***[7812] at his footstool.* (Psalms 132:7)

I will **worship** *[7812] toward thy holy temple, and praise thy name for thy loving kindness and for thy truth: for thou hast magnified thy word above all thy name.* (Psalms 138:2)

Their land also is full of idols; they __worship__[7812] the work of their own hands, that which their own fingers have made: (Isaiah 2:8)

In that day a man shall cast his idols of silver, and his idols of gold, which they made each one for himself to __worship__,[7812] to the moles and to the bats; (Isaiah 2:20)

And it shall come to pass in that day, that the great trumpet shall be blown, and they shall come which were ready to perish in the land of Assyria, and the outcasts in the land of Egypt, and shall __worship__[7812] the LORD in the holy mount at Jerusalem. (Isaiah 27:13)

But if thou say to me, We trust in the LORD our God: is it not he, whose high places and whose altars Hezekiah hath taken away, and said to Judah and to Jerusalem, Ye shall __worship__ before this altar? (Isaiah 36:7)

They lavish gold out of the bag, and weigh silver in the balance, and hire a goldsmith; and he makes it a god: they fall down, yea, they __worship__.[7812] (Isaiah 46:6)

Thus saith the LORD, the Redeemer of Israel, and his Holy One, to him whom man despises, to him whom the nation abhors, to a servant of rulers, Kings shall see and arise, princes also shall __worship__,[7812] because of the LORD that is faithful, and the Holy One of Israel, and he shall choose thee. (Isaiah 49:7)

*And it shall come to pass, that from one new moon to an-other, and from one sabbath to another, shall all flesh come to **worship**[7812] before me, saith the LORD.* (Isaiah 66:23)

*Stand in the gate of the LORD's house, and proclaim there this word, and say, Hear the word of the LORD, all ye of Ju-dah, that enter in at these gates to **worship**[7812] the LORD.* (Jeremiah 7:2)

*This evil people, which refuse to hear my words, which walk in the imagination of their heart, and walk after other gods, to serve them, and to **worship**[7812] them, shall even be as this girdle, which is good for nothing.* (Jeremiah 13:10)

*And go not after other gods to serve them, and to **worship**[7812] them, and provoke me not to anger with the of your hands; and I will do you no hurt.* (Jeremiah 25:6)

*Thus saith the LORD; Stand in the court of the LORD's house, and speak unto all the cities of Judah, which come to **worship**[7812] in the LORD's house, all the words that I command thee to speak unto them; diminish not a word:* (Jer. 26:2)

*And when we burned incense to the queen of heaven, and poured out drink offerings unto her, did we make her cakes to **worship**[6087] her, and pour out drink offerings unto her, without our men?* (Jeremiah 44:19)

And the prince shall enter by the way of the porch of that gate without, and shall stand by the post of the gate, and the priests shall prepare his burnt offering and his peace offerings, and he shall __worship__[7812] at the threshold of the gate: then he shall go forth; but the gate shall not be shut until the evening. (Ezekiel 46:2)

Likewise the people of the land shall __worship__[7812] at the door of this gate before the LORD in the sabbaths and in the new moons. (Ezekiel 46:3)

But when the people of the land shall come before the LORD in the solemn feasts, he that enters in by the way of the north gate to __worship__[7812] shall go out by the way of the south gate; and he that enters by the way of the south gate shall go forth by the way of the north gate: he shall not return by the way of the gate whereby he came in, but shall go forth over against it. (Ezekiel 46:9)

That at what time ye hear the sound of the cornet, flute, harp, sackbut, psaltery, dulcimer, and all kinds of music, ye

fall down and __worship__[5457] the golden image that Nebuchadnezzar the king hath set up: (Daniel 3:5)

Thou, O king, hast made a decree, that every man that shall hear the sound of the cornet, flute, harp, sackbut, psaltery, and dulcimer, and all kinds of music, shall fall down and __worship__[5457] the golden image: (Daniel 3:10)

There are certain Jews whom thou hast set over the affairs of \the province of Babylon, Shadrach, Meshach, and Abed-nego; these men, O king, have not regarded thee: they serve not thy gods, nor **worship**[5457] *the golden image which thou hast set up.* (Daniel 3:12)

Nebuchadnezzar spoke and said unto them, Is it true, O Shadrach, Meshach, and Abed-nego, do not ye serve my gods, nor **worship**[5457] *the golden image which I have set up?* (Daniel 3:14)

Now if ye be ready that at what time ye hear the sound of the cornet, flute, harp, sackbut, psaltery, and dulcimer, and all kinds of music, ye fall down and **worship**[5457] *the image which I have made; well: but if ye worship not, ye shall be cast the same hour into the midst of a burning fiery furnace; and who is that God that shall deliver you out of my hands?* (Daniel 3:15)

But if not be it known unto thee, O king, that we will not serve thy gods, nor **worship**[5457] *the golden image which thou hast set up.* (Daniel 3:18)

Then Nebuchadnezzar spoke, and said, Blessed be the God of Shadrach, Meshach, and Abed-nego, who hath sent his angel, and delivered his servants that trusted in him, and have changed the king's[4430] *word,*[4406] *and yielded their bodies, that they might not serve nor* **worship**[5457] *any god, ex-*

cept their own God. (Daniel 3:28)

*Thy graven images also will I cut off, and thy standing images out of the midst of thee; and thou shalt no more **worship**[7812] the work of thine hands.* (Micah 5:13)

*And them that **worship**[7812] the host of heaven upOn the housetops; and them that worship[7812] and that swear by the LORD, and that swear by Malcham;* (Zephaniah 1:5)

*The LORD will be terrible unto them: for he will famish all the gods of the earth; and men shall **worship**[7812] him, everyone from his place, even all the isles of the heathen.* (Zephaniah 2:11)

*And it shall come to pass, that every one that is left of all the nations which came against Jerusalem shall even go up from year to year to **worship**[7812] the King, the LORD of hosts, and to keep the feast of tabernacles.* (Zechariah 14:16)

*And it shall be, that whoso will not come up of all the families of the earth unto Jerusalem to **worship**[7812] the King, the LORD of hosts, even upon them shall be no rain.* (Zechariah 14:17)

OLD TESTAMENT DEFINITIONS FROM

STRONGS CONCORDANCE

H7812 shâchâh pronounced *shaw-khaw'*

A primitive root; to *depress*, that is, *prostrate* (especially reflexively in homage to royalty or God): - bow (self) down, crouch, fall down (flat), humbly beseech, do (make) obeisance, do reverence, make to stoop, worship.

H5457 s^egid pronounced *seg-eed'*

(Chaldee); corresponding to H5456: - worship.

H6087 'âtsab pronounced *aw-tsab'*

A primitive root; properly to *carve*, that is, *fabricate* or *fashion*; hence (in a bad sense) to *worry*, *pain* or *anger*: - displease, grieve, hurt, make, be sorry, vex, worship, wrest.

APPENDIX B

SCRIPTURE REFERENCES OF WORSHIP
New Testament

*Saying, Where is he that is born King of the Jews? for we have seen his star in the east, and are come to **worship**[4352] him.* (Matthew 2:2)

*And he sent them to Bethlehem, and said, Go and search diligently for the young child; and when ye have found him, bring me word again, that I may come and **worship**[4352] him also.* (Matthew 2:8)

*And saith unto him, All these things will I give thee, if thou wilt fall down and **worship**[4352] me.* (Matthew 4:9)

*Then saith Jesus unto him, Get thee hence, Satan: for it is written, Thou shalt **worship**[4352] the Lord thy God, and him only shalt thou serve.* (Matthew 4:10)

But in vain they do worship[4576] me, teaching for doctrines the commandments of men. (Matthew 15:9)

*Howbeit in vain do they **worship**[4576] me, teaching for doctrines the commandments of men.* (Mark 7:7)

*If thou therefore wilt **worship**[4352] me, all shall be thine.* (Luke 4:7)

*And Jesus answered and said unto him, Get thee behind me, Satan: for it is written, Thou shalt **worship**[4352] the Lord thy God, and him only shalt thou serve.* Luke 4:8)

*But when thou art bidden, go and sit down in the lowest room; that when he bade thee cometh, he may say unto thee, Friend, go up higher: then shalt thou have **worship**[1391] in the presence of them that sit at meat with thee.* (Luke 14:10)

*Our fathers worshiped[4352] in this mountain; and ye say, that in Jerusalem is the place where men ought to **worship**.[4352]* (John 4:20)

*Jesus saith unto her, Woman, believe me, the hour cometh, when ye shall neither in this mountain, nor yet at Jerusalem, **worship**[4352] the Father.* (John 4:21)

*Ye **worship**[4352] ye know not what: we know what we **worship**:[4352] for salvation is of the Jews.* (John 4:22)

*The hour cometh, and now is, when the true **worship-ers**[4353] shall **worship**[4352] the Father in spirit and in truth: the Father* *seeketh such to **worship**4352 him.* (John 4:23)

*God is a Spirit: and they that **worship**4352 him must **worship**4352 him in spirit and in truth.*225 (John 4:24)

*And there were certain Greeks among them that came up to **worship**4352 at the feast:* (John 12:20)

*Then God turned, and gave them up to **worship**3000 the host of heaven; as it is written in the book of the prophets, O ye house of Israel, have ye offered to me slain beasts and sacrifices by the space of forty years in the wilderness?* (Acts 7:42)

*Yea, ye took up the tabernacle of Moloch, and the star of your god Remphan, figures which ye made to **worship**4352 them: and I will carry you away beyond Babylon.* (Acts 7:43)

*And he arose and went: and, behold, a man of Ethiopia, an eunuch of great authority under Candace queen of the Ethiopians, who had the charge of all her treasure and had come to Jerusalem for to **worship**,4352* (Acts 8:27)

*For as I passed by, and beheld your devotions, I found an altar with this inscription, TO THE UNKNOWN GOD. Whom therefore ye ignorantly **worship**,2151 him declare I unto you.* (Acts 17:23)

Saying, This fellow *persuadeth men to **worship**4576 God* *contrary to the law.* (Acts 18:13)

Because that thou mayest understand, that there are yet but twelve days since I went up to Jerusalem for to wor-ship.⁴³⁵² (Acts 24:11)

But this I confess unto thee, that after the way which they call heresy, so worship³⁰⁰⁰ I the God of my fathers, believing all things which are written in the law and in the prophets: (Acts 24:14)

*And thus are the secrets of his heart made manifest; and so falling down on his face he will **worship**⁴³⁵² God, and report that God is in you of a truth.* (1 Corinthians 14:25)

*For we are the circumcision, which **worship**³⁰⁰⁰ God in the spirit, and rejoice in Christ Jesus, and have no confidence in the flesh.* (Philippians 3:3)

*Which things have indeed a show of wisdom in **will-worship**, and humility, and neglecting of the body; not in any honor to the satisfying of the flesh.* (Colossians 2:23)

*And again, when he bringeth in the first begotten into the world, he saith, And let all the angels of God wo**rship**⁴³⁵² him.* (Hebrews 1:6)

Behold, I will make them of the synagogue of Satan, which say they are Jews, and are not, but do lie; behold, I will make them to come and __worship__[4352] before thy feet, and to know that I have loved thee. (Revelation 3:9)

The twenty four elders fall down before him that sat on the throne, and __worship__[4352] him that lives forever and ever, and cast their crowns before the throne, saying, (Revelation 4:10)

And the rest of the men which were not killed by these plagues yet repented not of the works of their hands, that they should not __worship__[4352] devils, and idols of gold, and silver, and brass, and stone, and of wood: which neither can see, nor hear, nor walk: (Revelation 9:20)

And there was given me a reed like unto a rod: and the angel stood, saying, Rise, and measure the temple of God, and the altar, and them that __worship__[4352] therein. (Revelation 11:1)

And all that dwell upon the earth shall __worship__[4352] him, whose names are not written in the book of life of the Lamb slain from the foundation of the world. (Rev. 13:8)

And he exercises all the power of the first beast before him, and causes the earth and them which dwell therein to __worship__[4352] the first beast, whose deadly wound was healed. (Revelation 13:12)

And he had power to give life unto the image of the beast, that the image of the beast should both speak, and cause *that as many as would not **worship**[4352] the image of the beast should be killed.* (Revelation 13:15)

*Saying with a loud voice, Fear God, and give glory to him; for the hour of his judgment is come: and **worship**[4352] him that made heaven, and earth, and the sea, and the fountains of waters.* (Revelation 14:7)

*And the third angel followed them, saying with a loud voice, If any man **worship** the beast and his image, and receive his mark in his forehead, or in his hand,* (Revelation 14:9)

*And the smoke of their torment ascendeth up forever and ever: and they have no rest day nor night, who **worship**[4352] the beast and his image, and whosoever receiveth the mark of his name.* (Revelation 14:11)

*Who shall not fear thee, O Lord, and glorify thy name for thou only art holy: for all nations shall come and **worship** before thee; for thy judgments are made manifest.* (Revelation 15:4)

*And I fell at his feet to worship him. And he said unto me, See thou do it not: I am thy fellow servant, and of thy brethren that have the testimony of Jesus: **worship** God: for the testimony of Jesus is the spirit of prophecy.* (Revelation 19:10)

*And I John saw these things, and heard them. And when I had heard and seen, I fell down to **worship**[4352] before the* *feet of the angel which showed me these things.* (Revelation 22:8)

Then saith he unto me, See thou do it not: for I am thy fellow servant, and of thy brethren the prophets, and of them which keep the sayings of this book: **worship**[4352] *God.* (Revelation 22:9)

NEW TESTAMENT DEFINITIONS
FROM
STRONG'S CONCORDANCE

G4352 proskuneō pronounced *pros-koo-neh'-o*
From G4314 and probably a derivative of G2965 (meaning to *kiss*, like a dog *licking* his master's hand); to *fawn* or *crouch to*, that is, (literally or figuratively) *prostrate* oneself in homage (*do reverence* to, *adore*): - worship.

G3000 latreuō prounounced *lat-ryoo'-o*
From λάτρις latris (a hired *menial*); to *minister* (to God), that is, *render* religious *homage:* - serve, do the service, worship (-per).

G2151 eusebeō pronounced *yoo-seb-eh'-o*
From G2152; to *be pious*, that is, (towards God) to *worship*, or (towards parents) to *respect* (*support*): - show piety, worship.

MY PRAYER FOR YOU

Lord as I come to the end of this book, I thank you for bringing us fresh revelation as to what true worship is. I ask that this work will also bring the reader fresh revelation, so that they also will be Holy dissatisfied because they will know by Holy Spirit that there is far more of Kingdom manifestation to be appropriated in and through their life.

Father that we will come to believe that not only can we do the works Jesus did, but greater than He did because He told us that it is expedient for Him to depart so that we would have Holy Spirit walking with us and working in and through us.

I pray that as we learn to walk in obedience, not out of duty or fear, but Father out of love and intimacy thereby showing the lifestyle of worship that will be a witness to the sphere of influence you have been appointed to.

Father for those of us who have a "fear" of the word obedience due to bad experiences with authority figures in our lives because love was missing in the correction process who never understood the meaning of love and how correction with love is. Let them know that this day they are loved not by performance or obedience or disobedience, but in spite of it. So that from this day they will be free to walk out obedience because of their love for you, to honor you before all who see them walk out their destiny.

Holy Spirit seal in each heart that which each one would glean from this book, and that will enable each one to grow into the full measure of what you have designed them to be and to do. We know Father that as they grow they will do exploits, for you promised us that they that know their God shall do exploits.

In Jesus name I pray, Amen

NOTES:

NOTES:

NOTES:

<u>NOTES</u>:

TO SCHEDULE MINISTRY.

John is available to speak, if you want him for a seminar, conference or to minister in your church you may contact us at Schoolofthekingdom@gmail.com. with 'Ministry Schedule' in subject line.

He is also available to answer any questions you may have especially on the topic of the Kingdom of God. Send to schoolofthekingdom@gmail.com with 'Question' in the subject line he will answer as soon as possible..

OUR CONTACT INFORMATION

KINGDOM APOSTOLIC NETWORK
PO BOX 29, ASHLAND VA 23005

CELL (540) 435-0562

WEBSITES:
SCHOOLOFTHEKINGDOM.COM
KINGDOMLIVINGMEDIA.COM

COMING SOON:

KINGDOMLIVINGINTERNATIONAL.COM

PRODUCT PAGES
SINGLE CD TEACHING

Developing a Hebrew Mindset   **$8**

First Fruits   **$8**

Never Lay Down Your Vision   **$8**

Show Me Your Glory   **$8**

All prices include shipping in U.S

Make checks payable to: K-A-N

PO Box 29, Ashland VA 23005

Phone 540 435 0562

Email: Schoolofthekingdom@gmail.com

PRODUCT PAGES

CD TEACHING ALBUMS SMALL

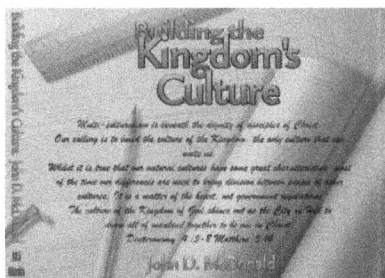

Pleasure Series [3 Cd's]   **$22**

Living Life with Passion [3 Cd's]   **$22**

Your Kingdom Identity [3 Cd's]   **$22**

Building the Kingdom Culture [3]   **$22**

All prices include shipping in U.S

Make checks payable to: K-A-N

PO Box 29, Ashland VA 23005

Phone 540 435 0562

Email: Schoolofthekingdom@gmail.com

PRODUCT PAGES
CD TEACHING ALBUMS LARGE

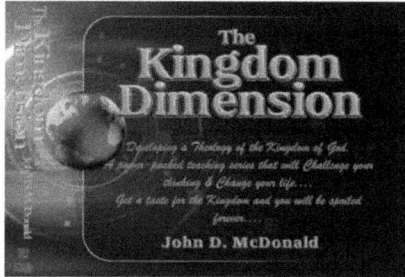

The Kingdom Dimension [14 Cd's] $89

Manifesting the Kingdom [9 Cd's] $65

The Journey of Faith   [9 Cd's] $65

Fuel For Revival   [8 Cd's] $59

All prices include shipping in U.S

Make checks payable to: K-A-N

PO Box 29, Ashland VA 23005

Phone 540 435 0562

Email: SchooloftheKingdom@gmail.com

ABOUT THE AUTHOR...
continued from back cover.

Commonwealth Bible College [AOG] now Southern Cross Bible College. Graduating in 1981 with a Diploma in Bible and Christian Ministries, in 1994 He graduated from Harvest Bible College, with a BA in Biblical Studies [Theology]

From the beginning of those teen years he gravitated to leaders and would silently listen to them. Only recently he understood his service in the Australian armed forces, conscripted in 1966 – 68, he was placed in the Catering Corps, as personal chef for his Battalion Commander, then within the Officers Mess, giving leaders the nourishment to be able to function in their service. The correlation in the spiritual realm is that he has been willing conscripted by the Lord to feed leaders in the body of Christ the Spiritual food to enable them to fulfill their calling.

Until his departure for America, John had

planted and pastored three churches in Australia.

It was during the illness of His wife, Jan, that the Lord began to take him on a journey of re-discovering the Kingdom. The more he studied the Biblical understanding of the kingdom, the more his thinking was challenged. It became a foundation of his teaching. Coming to the US, he was directed of the Lord to focus on 'revival' and so began to teach from that perspective. It was in 2003 that the Lord began to get him to refocus on the Kingdom; also at the same time, he confessed his failure to accepting his apostolic call. At that moment, things changed even though he knew at an early age that he had an apostolic calling; [although that is not what is was called back then] he would not accept it due to seeing so much 'leadership abuse' in the church.

It was early 2004 that a joint statement was issued from the prophetic elders. Although it was not a personal prophetic word, it was confirming the direction I was going. The one passage that was confirmation was this: God is now raising up Apostles and Prophets who will bring fresh revelation of the Kingdom of God.

John has leaders who look to him for counsel because they want to tap the depth of wisdom and knowledge God has given him. He is considered a mentor and a spiritual father.

Church planting passion, whilst being on the back burner for some years, is being stirred again. There are two reasons he believes this is so. Firstly, to build a renew model others can be part of, a model that raises sons to go and build their own ministry and churches, and for those who have an apostolic call, their own resource centers, a First Century model for the 21st Century Church.

Secondly, having a successful model that others can use enlarges the sphere of one's influence and has a more effective home base to help other servants of the Lord. When we are focused on the kingdom, we recognize the body of Christ, no matter what name tag one has on the door. This is discerning the Lord's body, commanded so that together we can walk in an abundant life, the lifestyle and culture of the Kingdom.

---

www.ingramcontent.com/pod-product-compliance
Lightning Source LLC
Chambersburg PA
CBHW061829040426
42447CB00012B/2884